Watch It Grow

Watch a Strawberry Grow

by Kirsten Chang

Bullfrog Books

Ideas for Parents and Teachers

Bullfrog Books let children practice reading informational text at the earliest reading levels. Repetition, familiar words, and photo labels support early readers.

Before Reading

- Discuss the cover photo. What does it tell them?
- Look at the picture glossary together. Read and discuss the words.

Read the Book

- "Walk" through the book and look at the photos. Let the child ask questions. Point out the photo labels.
- Read the book to the child, or have him or her read independently.

After Reading

- Prompt the child to think more. Ask: Do you like to eat strawberries? Can you explain how they grow?

Bullfrog Books are published by Jump!
5357 Penn Avenue South
Minneapolis, MN 55419
www.jumplibrary.com

Library of Congress Cataloging-in-Publication Data

Names: Chang, Kirsten, 1991- author.
Title: Watch a strawberry grow / by Kirsten Chang.
Description: Minneapolis, MN: Jump!, [2019]
Series: Watch it grow | Includes index.
Identifiers: LCCN 2018022600 (print)
LCCN 2018029589 (ebook)
ISBN 9781641282666 (ebook)
ISBN 9781641282642 (hardcover: alk. paper)
ISBN 9781641282659 (pbk.)
Subjects: LCSH: Strawberries—Juvenile literature.
Classification: LCC SB385 (ebook) | LCC SB385 .C43 2019 (print) | DDC 634/.75—dc23
LC record available at https://lccn.loc.gov/2018022600

Editor: Jenna Trnka
Designer: Michelle Sonnek

Photo Credits: matin/Shutterstock, cover; Henrik Larsson/Shutterstock, 1; Alex Staroseltsev/Shutterstock, 3, 6–7, 22t; Boris Bulychev/Shutterstock, 4; Mary Lynn Strand/Shutterstock, 5; Wstockstudio/Shutterstock, 8, 23br; trigga/iStock, 9; ID1974/Shutterstock, 10–11, 22mr, 23bm; Volodymyr Nikitenko/Shutterstock, 12–13, 23bl; Khalangot Sergey L/Shutterstock, 14–15, 22br; AN NGUYEN/Shutterstock, 16, 22bl; Sanit Fuangnakhon/Shutterstock, 17, 22ml, 23tm; Fei Yang/Getty, 18–19; Sergii Chepulskyi/Shutterstock, 20–21; Andrii Koval/Shutterstock, 23tl; Jiang Zhongyan/Shutterstock, 23tr; Iurii Kachkovskyi/Shutterstock, 24.

Printed in the United States of America at Corporate Graphics in North Mankato, Minnesota.

Table of Contents

Red Fruit

Roy loves to eat strawberries.

Where do they come from?

A strawberry
starts as a seed.

It is tiny!

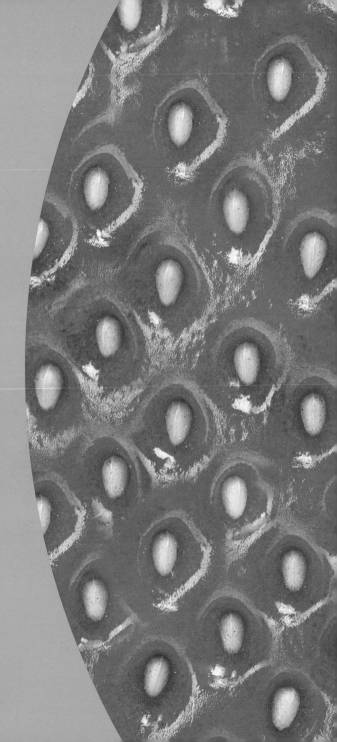

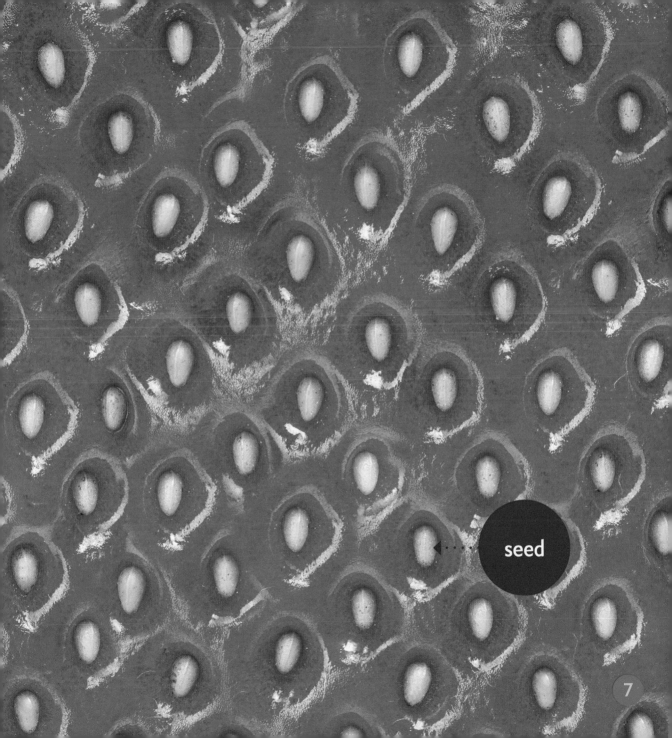

seed

The seed is
planted in soil.

It grows into a seedling.
The young plant
needs lots of sunlight.

The roots grow.

The leaves grow.

The plant
grows runners.

runner

bee

flower

Look! Flowers!

Bees fly from
flower to flower.

They take pollen
with them.

This helps the
fruit grow.

It is a strawberry!

When the fruit
is red, it is ripe.

It is ready
to be picked.

We go to a farm.

We pick our own fruit.

Yum! We love
strawberries.

Life Cycle of a Strawberry

How does a strawberry grow?

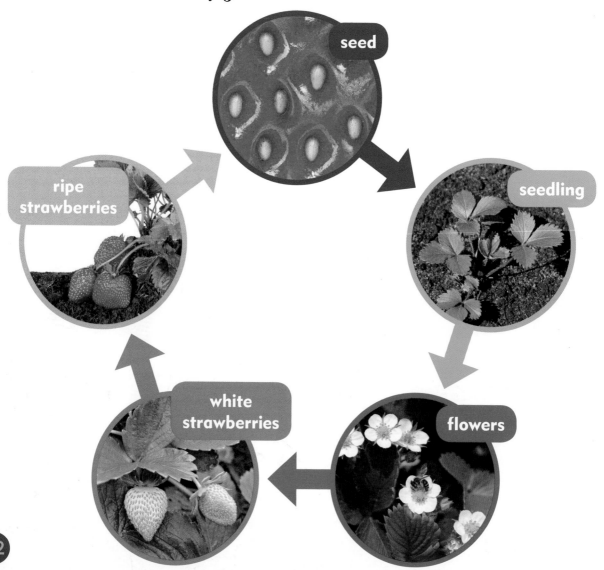

seed

seedling

ripe strawberries

flowers

white strawberries

Picture Glossary

pollen
Tiny yellow grains that cause plants to form seeds.

ripe
Fully grown and ready to eat.

roots
Parts of a plant that grow underground and get water and food from the soil.

runners
Thin stems that grow from the base of a plant.

seedling
A young plant grown from a seed.

soil
Another word for dirt.

Index

To Learn More

Learning more is as easy as 1, 2, 3.

1) Go to www.factsurfer.com

2) Enter "watchastrawberrygrow" into the search box.

3) Click the "Surf" button to see a list of websites.

With factsurfer.com, finding more information is just a click away.